DON'T CALL HIM RETARDED!

I cared for him over 20 years.

D1728222

Don't Call Him Retarded
© 2022 by Camelia Wall

ISBN 978-0-9967997-3-7

Published by:
Godly Writes Publishing
P. O. Box 2005
Orangeburg SC 29116-2005

Cover design by Greg Jackson, ThinkPen Design

For Worldwide Distribution. Printed in the U.S.A.

DON'T CALL HIM RETARDED!

I cared for him over 20 years.

CAMELIA WALL

Table of Contents

Introduction

THE PURPOSE FOR THIS MANUSCRIPT

The intent behind the creation of this manual was not simply to provide a good read filled with real life dramas complete with and unsuspected conclusion. My reason for producing this script could very well have been to tell the story of how Alec became family or to leave my thoughts beyond my grave, or to shed light on/expose a system of things that have been designed to help a people who in most cases or not quite able to help themselves, a system originally established with good intent, a system created to assist other individuals with living their best life. A system, when viewed through a clear lens is severely out of focus. Contrary to its original purpose.

My intent is to give insight into the system of this institution in connection to real life experience and how to overcome its built- in flaws. This insight, in fact, can be employed daily, not just within the DDSN or the DHHS system but within the system of life by allowing GOD, the Creator of heaven and earth, to not only strengthen us with tenacity and bless us with HIS wisdom and power but also to guide us by His Spirit.

Additionally. the purpose is to introduce potential caregivers to this type of system, but also to introduce the larger community to what is involved and to tell a personal story as an indication of why this is a necessary offering by society for people who are people whom we must help.

Chapter One

ROUTINE PROCEDURE

> *It's a new morning. Thank You, for strengthening me*
> *for the day ahead. Thank You for protection, divine*
> *guidance, and the favor that surrounds my family*
> *and me like a shield this day! You are good, Abba!*

Yes! Another day that I have been granted the privilege of sight, sound, smell, touch, and by far my favorite of them all taste. My thoughts, as always seem to be all over the place from, "What should I wear?" to "Who do I need to call?" to "Where do I need to be?" to "What's for dinner tonight?"

"Breakfast! I've got to have some of that as well."

In our daily living, we tend to cart ourselves around like robots with never-ending thoughts. Even when we slow down to take the much-deserved power nap, our minds continue to press onward. In that case, is it rest?

Mondays through Fridays are more demanding, like the weekends, and the weekends more like a blink of the eye. I have a husband and two young adults to care for, and I additionally look after my buddy, my "task," Alec, also playfully referred to at times as "Dude." Alec, who has somehow managed the art of being both a joy and a challenge for me. How he developed the skill of helping me remain in a desperate, wondrous state of being, may be somewhat attributed to my DNA. Alec is not a biological member of the family, but he is by every right a family member. He is the family that we choose.

Alec, a 65-year-old male, ward of the state, who has lived with my family for over two decades. He is intellectually challenged, legally blind, deaf, mute, and diabetic and shows signs of having some form of dementia. He was never taught to sign, nor does he respond to chatter of any sort. The rhetorical question I often received from laymen and professionals alike is "How do you communicate with him?" My reply? "We just do."

I can't very easily articulate how that's done, so I cut through the core very quickly, making that long story short with a proper response: "Time has afforded the two of us the ability to do so, and we do—that is, we communicate."

In the beginning, trust was a big concern for all of us. Alec and I needed time to know and understand one another, This learning curve is a never-ending journey for the entire family, in fact. My first thought when asked to take on the responsibility for another member of the family, and such a potentially difficult one, was that we had young children in the home. Having children in the home and allowing a stranger into the house was something my husband and I gave quite serious consideration.

Reminiscing, I recall I had by then accepted Jesus into my life as Savior. But assuredly, I had not yet given Him Lordship over the details of my life. In all honesty, I don't know where I was relative to my thought process at the time when we were determining whether to accept Alec into our home and provide him with a much-needed service. I don't recall whether my husband and I had sense enough to commune with God concerning what we were contemplating.

Whatever our thought process was, my husband and I decided that we would step out into the water. We did so. We accepted Alec into our home. I won't tell you that the decision was an easy one to make. I will tell you that once we went through the initial turbulence of unfamiliarity all was well. For a short time anyway.

Father, how grateful I am that You love us all with a never-ending love! I need do no searching of your understanding. Your faithfulness toward us is immeasurable, and your FAVOR surrounds us like a shield. Thank you, JESUS for paving the path for me to be in the right relationship with Abba, our Father. Thank you for allotting my family the courage to step out into the uncertain depth of waters where we have found that our omnipresent heavenly FATHER has awarded us blessings that can be surpassed by HIM alone. Thank you, Father. To give thanks unto the LORD and to sing praises unto HIS name is good.

Alec temperament seems to be pleasant most of the time. He smiles and laughs out loud. He likes to sit in front of the television whether it has a picture on it or not, so long as it's powered on. He enjoys the sunshine better than rainy days. The sun seems to contribute to his ability to see better than on a cloudy day. Like most of our family, Alec enjoys a good meal, though because of his ability to eat lightning fast, I sometimes wonder if he's tasting his food.

Initially, Alec appeared to have been provided nothing prior to being brought into our home. He had some clothing, mostly secondhand, a fact evident by someone's name other than Alec's being written on the items in magic marker. He had a t-shirt, a few undergarments, some new socks and so on. Although I wasn't aware of it at first, I learned early on that Alec had a keen instinct for survival. He managed to get his hands on a pair of Ron's (my husband's) favorite Levi's. That was what tipped me off that Alec had good taste in clothing.

When retrieving the Levi's, I happened upon several other articles of clothing that belonged to my husband. My thought was *Clothing is always washed separately here, so how did he manage to accomplish this without being noticed?* In his own way, Alec was quite the artist. Yes, the artistry of thievery. Alec was stealing.

We attended the state fair and while standing at a vendor making a decision as to what we would purchase, I saw Alec and another buddy snatch a bottled water from inside the vendor's window. Yes, he reached into the window and grabbed the bottled water. The vendor yelled, "H*ey! come back here.*"

Both Alec and his partner in crime attempted a quick escape. I mentioned earlier that Alec is legally blind. It's pointless to mention, but I'm going to mention it anyway. He didn't get very far. We confiscated the water and returned it to the vendor with the apology that was in order. Of course, I was the one who returned that bottled water and issue the apology. Although I'm certain the vendor didn't realize that her thief was blind, she could see that Alec functioned with a handicap. She accepted my apology and let the matter go.

Although this conduct was very serious and at the same time very funny, I noted that a change in this kind of behavior was necessary. I would like to add that from the very beginning, many matters were going on at the same time that were concerning, relative to the placement of Alec with our family. We had days when I felt as if our taking him into our home wasn't going to work.

In fact, the persons who had originally spoken with my husband and me in an attempt to persuade us to consider this man's plight, assured us that Alec was a high-functioning individual with a loving personality, and that all would be well. Further they reassured me that in cases that may not be well, they, my knights of shimmering armor, would be there for both Alec and me.

Promises of assistance whenever needed were made: respite, transportation, help with appointments, day-programs services, working together as a team in order to achieve a common goal. My understanding of the established goal was to serve our mentally and physically disable community. Great- peace and tranquility. We were meant to serve our targeted consumers under the designation of direct support professional or caregiver, whichever title you prefer. I'll also use the acronym DSP in place of the title direct support professional.

At moments, I shared certain information with individuals whom I often referred to as the *"knights of the round table,"* or *"the powers that be."* Or, better, yet those individuals who think they be *"the power".* Often, I felt as though the information I was sharing in attempting to achieve our common goal of servicing the client was being used against me. Wow! *What is going on here? Where is that promised teamwork? Who are you people? Where are my knights?*

> *Every way of a man is right in his own eyes:*
> *but the LORD looks upon the hearts.*
> *Father, allow the words from my mouth and the*
> *meditation of my heart to be acceptable in your*
> *sight. You are my strength and my redeemer:*

You know, I should mention that I had reasons for accepting Alec into our home other than that they ask me to. We as a family had recently relocated from Texas to the state of South Carolina. I didn't know much about this state and although I had obtained work, I had two very young children and my preference was to be readily available to them in their infant and toddler stages. Even though I have never said this out loud, somehow in my mind I felt that raising young children to contribute to society, teaching them to work hard to produce prosperity with a purpose wasn't enough. Accepting Alec would help me to feel as if I was more productive in society.

My husband and I had several discussions regarding the subject. We decided that Alec would primarily be my responsibility, as my husband was bombarded with the responsibility of life issues relative to the entire home. Often, I use the term "me"; however, my husband is definitely here, although he doesn't complete the paperwork. Oh yes, *"paperwork."* That leads me back to the subject of my "knights in shimmering armor."

During a scheduled appointment with one of the shimmering knights, I asked why was I not given certain information relative to Alec, and on the other hand, why was I provided with information that does not seem to be accurate? They had assured me he was high functioning with a few limitations. I will tell you that this information was not coming across as accurate at all. Nonetheless I was made to feel as if either I would adhere to the commitment or they will find someone else to do the work.

So, I reasoned with myself because people who have full intellectual functioning have behaviors, training can fix this.

From the beginning I believe that I saw Alec as a person with some cognitive limitations. Deep down within me I probably whispered, *"That's all. We can fix that."* When Alec and family went into our first restaurant together, for instance, I never imagined he would refuse to sit down.

What's the matter? It's only a table. Have a seat. He refused. We allowed him to continue to stand. Whatever his pleasure.

The thought had never dawned on me before this day that in the United States of America in the year of 2001, a grown man had never experienced the pleasure of being served a meal in a restaurant. Wow! I was faced with a realization. I'd been living in my on little reality. We have people in our civilization that through no fault of their own have never had the experience of dining in a restaurant.

I will say that once the food was brought to our table, Alec had a change of mind. He sat down.

I thought, *He'll be okay. He just needs some time and attention.* A tad bit of basic training on things such as, restaurant etiquette, wiping off his shoes prior to entering into the living area, covering his mouth when he sneezes, utilizing personal need items, slowing down at the dinner table, closing a bathroom door when inside, not eating food off the floor, and the inappropriateness of walking through the house in the nude.

On occasion, when Alec dislike things or became aggravated, he would communicate a state of irritation by the removal of his clothing. The fact that he was in public view was of no concern to him.

At times, Alec's only way of letting me know that he'd like to go to the restroom was to unzip is pants. He did that publicly as well. Okay, I am all for the right to do as you wish as long as no danger of any kind is involved. I also have a belief in the term "*appropriate behavior.*" On those days when he seemed as if he was never going to "get it," I felt as though he was lacking tremendously in his ability to comprehend.

As I reminisce, I suppose that in my own way I was attempting to turn him into my type of *normal.* I pondered thoughts of getting out quick, while at the same time doing what I could to "*hang in there... stay the course... don't quit.*" All the while, I was wondering whether I could handle this responsibility.

I believe we all should be allowed to exercise our rights, being able to express ourselves and enjoy our life at least to some degree. Yet, the unzipping of the pants regardless of who was standing there, or eating food off the floor in Walmart were some things Alec was simply not going to continue doing.

LORD, I need your wisdom and guidance
as to how I can resolve these matters.
I believe that in life rushing to judgement or being quick in
decision making especially when that decision can affect
the livelihood of a person with great magnitude is not
good. Proverbs refers to one who is quick to wrath as a
"fool" and one who is slow to anger as a "wise man" Bless
me with revelation knowledge in these matters, Father.

Chapter Two

DAYLIGHT FINALLY ARRIVES

Time went by and I began to recognize that Alec had more under-standing than I. My revelation started when I stood still in my home one day and watched my son, Chance, who at that time was just starting to walk on his own, stumble and fall.

Alec was then on his way into the bathroom, and my son happened to stumble right in front of Alec. I stood lifeless, just observing to see what my son would do after his fall. I was awed to witness Alec approach Chance. As he did so he stopped, bent over, and picked Chance up, placed him on his feet, set himself in motion around Chance and proceeded on his way into the lavatory.

What! Are you kidding me? Pardon my colloquialisms. I saw that I had been *"played"* consistently by the likes of Alec. This was a game changer.

To this day, I do not believe that Alec saw me standing there observing. My belief is that had Alec noted my presence, he would not have acknowledged my son taking a tumble at all. I will add that timing was key especially in such moments, as I don't know what my thought process would have been had I not witnessed the scenario from its beginning.

Yes, a slight glimmer of sun was surfacing our way. A form of rev-elation knowledge had advanced toward me. Alec had an ability to comprehend, after all. That observation that he placed Chance back on his feet and proceeded around him was for me a glistening light.

Time moved on. Alec began to show signs of putting forth an effort to communicate with us. He did things such as hold his hand out to me. Not sure what he wanted, I gave him what we call "*five*" which some refer to as a "*pound.*" Regardless of the jargon, it appeared at such a moment that he is satisfied with my reply. His response was discernable because he pulled his hand back and strutted on his way. Clearly his answer was in his step.

At times during breakfast or dinner, he will do a little dance with his feet up under our nook. I can only assume this conduct communicates that whatever he is engaging at that moment is soothing his palate. Nonetheless, barriers are surely being removed. The house has now become a home for Alec.

> *GOD is always aware. HE knows the outcome of*
> *a matter before it even begins. HE is LORD.*

I'm certain that I now have a better understanding of what's meant by the phrase "*a new day is dawning.*" All is good right now. I have a new revelation. What I felt to be a lack of comprehension ability for Alec, I began to recognize as a mode of defense. Remember, he is equipped with cognitive limitations that include but are not limited to blindness, mutism, deafness, intellectual disability, etc., etc.

The immediate rationale of most individuals I've introduced to Alec is that he is a person who, from an initial appearance is trapped inside himself. He has little to no sight. He is unable to hear or verbally articulate his needs or desires.

But the way I see him he has developed an ability to defend himself by using what seems to be his cognitive limitations. Alec has his own way of thinking. He decides when and whom he will trust.

Once you have been deemed trustworthy, he will begin to allow you into his world. That's when those defense mechanisms start to come down. The soul trusted by Alec can than experience the attribute of tenderness that his personality actually demonstrates.

Our FATHER in heaven is good to all HE has created

I finally thought to review Alec's personal files where I found contact information for his biological family. I reached out to them by way of a telephone call. Wow! I couldn't believe it! I was able to speak directly with his mom. At first she was somewhat standoffish, and rightfully so. I was a complete stranger. Here I was trying to speak with her regarding a son who had been raised as a ward of the state.

Time went on during our talk. She opened up a little. I had taken a few photographs of Alec. I asked, "W*ould you like me to send you a picture?*" She replied, "Y*es,*" and I did so. I didn't however, receive any feedback from her in response to the pictures I had sent.

A year or two later, though, lo and behold, I had a call from a family member of Alec's. The man introduced himself as Arthur, the oldest brother. He asked if I was the one who'd sent the pictures. I answered that I was. He told me that he was at his mother's house visiting from up North. He asked if it would be okay for him to come and see his brother. Of course, my reply was yes. We set up a day. I received the call on a Saturday, which I remember vividly. His family members would come to see him the next day. We stayed home from church that day, awaiting their arrival.

Alec's mother, the older brother (Arthur), a younger brother, a sister-in-law, a few children and their mom, came to see Alec on that Sunday. A little while after that visit, I learned that Alec's mom had been diagnosed with cancer. She lost her battle with the disease shortly after her visit with him.

Alec's older brother, Mr. Arthur, and I established a mutual business relationship. Arthur called often to check in on his brother, to see how things were going with him. He would always express his appreciation of the care provided to Alec through me and my family. Arthur would make comments such as," *Alec got himself a nice family.*" He would go on to tell me that he promised their mom to keep in contact, to keep up with Alec.

I was glad to hear that. Having the support of biological family members in most cases is good. Biological family is a source outside of the established system. Normally, they can speak regarding the person under care with little or no hesitance. They can make decisions concerning legal matters for their sibling or kindred. They can also help strengthen their family member's choice making position, giving the person in question more liberty to exercise their basic rights.

Biological family can also speak to the time, attention, and care afforded their kindred to maintain a good lifestyle, whereas the stance of someone in my position (contracted) in support of Alec maybe disregarded, ignored, or overlooked.

Please allow me to mention here that we live in a sadly degraded society. We can come in contact with a sort of wickedness daily at any given time. The foster care system is no different. A level of underhandedness exists even within such a well-intended system

The person doing mischief doesn't necessarily have to be the coordinator of a program. The wrongdoer can very well be an outside piece of the puzzle. A licensing entity with its own agenda can disrupt a carefully thought-out plan. God's word tells me where sin abounds, though, that grace abounds that much more, and abundantly. What am I saying? If you're drafted into the family of GOD through HIS Son, JESUS, you're a winner.

I have witnessed the powers that think they *be* attempt to manipulate relatives who come forth to advocate for family. Why would they do that? you ask. Generally, in my opinion for the sake of filthy lucre (money, in short) or old-fashion spite. That's my opinion.

Chapter Three

GOD REVEALS

Everywhere that I go, I always make a statement habitually, sometimes out loud and sometimes only within myself. That statement is, *I have got to be who I am. I have got to be who GOD made me to be.* That to me is one of the easiest things to do, be myself.

My model has been that if at any time you are not allowed to be who GOD created you to be, but instead you're persuaded to be something or someone you are not regardless of the reasoning, the situation is hard. I'm not saying that life will or should always be easy, but I am saying that for me the easiest thing is being myself.

What does *be myself* mean to me? That depends on the circumstances that I'm dealing with in that moment. I have a kind of complex scenario in mind, however. Although I am adamant about the *being myself* statement, to live is to learn. At times, certainly change is good and necessary, though I find that change is seldom welcomed by any of us. And the catch here is that no one can be certain whether a change is for the better (or not) until they agree to make that change.

I reviewed the state of affairs in relationship to Alec. I noted that I was guilty of trying to change him. I wanted him to be *normal,* like me. The nerve of me to call myself normal. I was going to *"fix him."* Make him a better person so that he might live a more fulfilling life. I made sure he obtained prescription eyeglasses and a hearing aid, both of which he refused to wear. His hearing was tested with the hearing aid on and Alec's brain waves indicated that he could then hear. Yet he refused to comply with wearing the assistive technology. How could that be? Everyone wants to be able to hear.

These types of things disappointed me. I was only trying to help him. I thought that his being able to hear would allow for a more satisfactory life. Again, the medical professionals assured me Alec could hear with the hearing aid on. Nonetheless, he never once responded to any verbal interactions while wearing that hearing aid. In due course he would remove it.

Eventually, I woke up to the truth of the matter. He had no desire to be equipped with aids relative to his eyesight or hearing. Doctors noted that Alec had functioned from childhood into adulthood without the use of such aids. Most likely at this point in his life, he felt no need for them. He would have probably adjusted to them better had he been given access from childhood.

Sometimes disappointments are part of life. I realized I was helping by getting in his way. Alec was being himself. For me this was a revelation. He functioned without the use of assistive technology. *Why should I want him to change?* I had to come to terms with this and moved forward. I left the aids in his possession, but I never again concerned myself with his choice not to use them.

Alec attends a day program a few hours a day. Monday thru Friday. He rises religiously just before daybreak to prepare himself. On the weekends, he rises at daybreak so to dress himself and wait for the family to get up. On any normal morning, the majority of the house is not up by daybreak. Alec functions on an independent basis relative to the days of the week. He is able to differentiate the days of the week from the weekends.

As far as the day program I 'm not certain why it is referred to as a *program*. Based on personal observation, Alec does nothing while there. He sits in a chair of his choice and rocks his head back and forth. Inclusive of a lunch and a few bathroom breaks, that is the majority of the *program.* Nonetheless, he appears to look forward to it. Alec enjoys his *program.*

Medical professionals will never be able to truly grasp the mind of Alec. He has days when he is just what one would refer to as a *regular Joe*, even with the cognitive limitations. Alec is a person who is as normal an individual as any. On other days, then his state of mind changes. This by all accounts is normal for each one of us. What is more, society itself is faulty. We all come equipped with some sort of mental disparity.

Alec has been 30 seconds from a private bathroom but will prefer to choose the outdoor grass area to relieve himself. He has also, oppositely, cleared his throat and rid himself of the resulting mucus by way of the bathroom commode. An explanation can't always be provided for certain occurrences except to say *he made a choice.* Sometimes in society we don't always make good choices. What is needed in the moment may well be a correction.

On paper, Alec is described as a mentally retarded/deficient person who is mute, deaf, and legally blind. He is a diabetic. Not long ago he had a lapse as to his identity and his location. He didn't know me or my husband. We took him to the emergency room where we explained the episode to his attending emergency room physician. All his lab work was good, and there was no sign of Stroke. Alec was cleared and released with medical documentation asking that he follow up with his primary care doctor. We pursued the follow up, and gave the information about the episode to the primary care physician. The primary physician also completed lab tests, which concluded Alec was clear.

I will mention that the emergency room physician as well as Alec's primary care doctor both seemed hesitant to say d*ementia.* I am certain, nonetheless, the episode showed signs of dementia.

In writing Alec appears to have a limited life base. Still his behaviors most of the time indicates him to be very fulfilled. He's always smiling and laughing out loud while simultaneously scratching his head. He has a personality that will cause an entire room full of people to smile, although they may not be sure of what they're smiling about. Nothing wrong with that.

Laughter does the body good like a medicine.

All in the family were well and appeared to be happy. We were having a smooth session. Everyone and everything going according to schedule. Our house was now a home.

One morning, all the family went their own ways. My husband was at work. The children were at school. Alec had gone to the workshop. The phone rang.

The voice on the other end proceeded to ask for me; "Speaking," I replied. This individual began to let me know that one of their knights had received a report that Alec was locked outside of the house this very morning and left home alone to wait for his transportation to the workshop. The accusation didn't even make sense to me. I think I jumped outside myself.

The knight proceeded to explain that Alec was being removed from my home due to an allegation. Further, the allegation would be investigated. The outcome of the investigation then would determine whether or not Alec would be allowed to return. In my mind, I screamed, a*re you serious? What are you talking about? You are all crazy*. I'm pretty sure my thoughts went something like that. Nevertheless, Alec was moved.

Although I don't think that the knights where aware of it, the emergency respite family communicated with me to ask me about behaviors and make me aware of certain things that had been happening while Alec was staying in their home. I didn't say much to the respite family. I'm certain they knew.

Alec wasn't aware of exactly what was happening. He wanted to come home. Unable to express this feeling verbally, the behaviors expressed it for him. Alec was then moved a couple of times during the investigation for reasons unknown to me.

To this very day, I have no certainty as to the exact chain of events that occurred causing him to be abruptly removed from his home on that day. I believe that the outcome of the matter was that there was a misunderstanding of a verbal communication between transportation personnel and one of the knights. Once the Department of Social Services completed its investigation, Alec was allowed to return home.

I know that most would say that the thoughts I had in connection to the abrupt removal of Alec from his home are called conspiracy theories. However, that doesn't matter to me. Name it what you want to. I call it discernment.

I gave thought to events that proceeded his removal and the drama associated with it. Thinking back, I recalled certain conversations and how I had received unsolicited phone calls accompanied by useless banter. The talk had nothing to do with Alec's wellbeing. No real intent had ever been made to permanently put Alec into a family environment. No real goal had ever been established to allow him a more fulfilled lifestyle.

When we were asked to accept Alec as a placement into our home, I'm unable to say with 100 percent certainty what the real intent was concerning his placement. Whatever the underlying motive, the consideration was not for him to have a more fulfilled life. Nonetheless, I came to terms with the belief that the goal was to place him with a family but not on a permanent basis.

Placing him with a family would justify proceeding forward with other factors associated with the placement. I don't believe that the intent of *the powers that think they be* was ever to permanently place him with a family.

Alec was out of his home for approximately 3 month pending conclusion of the investigation.

> *How is it that we always forget THE GOD FACTOR? HE*
> *is a tangible GOD. True and living, high and exalted.*

Meanwhile, something happened. Knights who had been instrumental in Alec's placement were exposed for exploitation of the state residents they should have been servicing. This instigated another inquiry. This investigation was due to the accusation involving a knight accused of exploitation. The knight, while being question relative to the charge, became agitated and abruptly removed himself from questioning. This knight who was of director- level status, never returned to his position. No further mention of him or the circumstances regarding his departure was made.

Although the organization did what it could to keep the matter of the investigation quiet, people talk. If they can't find out what they want to know, they draw their own conclusions. The consensus was that the director was being questioned in connection to the inappropriate treatment of several of our special needs consumers. The man became uncomfortable with the question-and-answer process and abruptly quit.

> *Every way of a man seems right in his own*
> *eyes but their end is destruction.*

Chapter Four

HOME AGAIN

Once Alec returned home, I instinctively felt as though his behavior toward me was somewhat suspect. He seemed almost to think I somehow had something to do with what he had just recently experienced. Though I made attempts to express to him that the unfortunate circumstances didn't occur due to any choice of mine, the physical limitations Alec comes equipped with didn't allot me the assurance that he understood what I was attempting to convey. Nevertheless, wounds heal in time as long as the scabs are left alone.

I can't imagine what being abruptly removed from any type home environment must feel like, but to be removed from a good home environment where you are familiar with the surroundings and feeling safe and comfortable, loving your life—then in a blink, your shifted to an environment where seemingly no one cares or is able to explain to in terms you understand, what's happening must be overwhelming.

I'm unable to tell you what it must have been like for Alec in that moment, but I can tell you that when I mulled over this situation in my mind, the realization was scary. During the slavery period, slaves would be sold off at will by their owners. The separated families experienced devastation. Thoughts of these occurrences to say the least are crushingly disturbing. That is the closes I could come to understanding what was happening to Alec in the instant they removed him.

Continuing straightway ahead as the hours, days, weeks, and months rolled by, Alec began to relax and trust again.

So once more we were family. I can think of a great many fascinating stories I could share with you concerning Alec. We've had some great fun. We've had what I would call *moments*. The entire household enjoys a good funny. Especially at the expense of someone other than oneself. Joy and laughter are two of the greatest partners that exist. We have certainly had some joyous times in this house. We have laughed to the point we were unable to laugh any more, but there's still some funny left in our thoughts, so now we had laughter till it hurt.

My children who were very young at the time, thought that everything Alec did was hilarious, from eating his dinner faster than speed racer to the out-loud inappropriate belch that followed as the encore. The immediate question posed to him in those moments usually, "A*re you kidding me?*" As I proceed to explain to him proper table etiquette, for whatever reason, this would make the matter even funnier. The thing is, the belch was out loud. Alec facial expression never changed. The effect was as if he didn't realize that I heard it.

Now, let me add that in no way would I ever condone this action. When such a breach occurred, a training opportunity ensued. I absolutely did not see any humor in it. But now when we look back on that as well as other situations we laugh and laugh and laugh. The memories have become precious. Who would have ever imagined such a thing? Certainly not me.

Clothed with strength and dignity she will laugh in the days to come.

Chapter Five

A CONFLICTED SYSTEM

Years went on and suddenly some changes were made administratively. These changes call for Alec to transition from what is referred to as one provider to another. Provider of what I still haven't figured out. For system paperwork purposes, Alec has been switched over from one set of knights to another set of knights. I myself experienced no changes. I remain responsible for all emotional, physical, and spiritual labor. I was not privy to why they had a need to make an administrative change.

What was more, Alec was not asked anything regarding preference in connection to his *right* to make an *informed decision*. That information was only made available to the knights at the round table.

What I do know is that a group of adult foster care persons being serviced within the general public were moved to a new set of knights. My position didn't change. Alec is still with me seven days a week. At the time of the switchover, my thoughts were: *Maybe I can get some help with servicing*. Nevertheless, as time moved on, I could see no chance of that happening with this new provider. My thought then was: *out of the frying pan straight into the fire*.

I realize that people mean well most of the time. When decisions are fashioned, I would like to believe that they are done so with the best of intentions—meaning, in hope that everything will work together for the good of all involved. I would like to be working within a program where I can consistently think optimistically. Being up close and acquiring firsthand knowledge of nonsense, foolishness, buffoonery, in the company of ethically challenged persons, thinking regularly in a positive vein is for me a challenge.

Does any of this jargon sound familiar? *Person Centered Planning, Personal Outcomes, Consumers have rights.* Again, people mean well. Some people also may start out meaning well, but they're tore down by obstacles set before them at the hands of people whose signatures are required.

On a large scale, these individuals have neither direct experience nor the acquired knowledge necessary to confidently execute paperwork they are signing off on. A signature oftentimes can make life-changing decisions on behalf of people they know nothing about.

Let me go back to *consumers have rights*; this statement is often thrown around in the adult foster care arena. In fact, some pride themselves at its constant usage. I guess that originally someone in administration said it. The phrase sounded good. They ran with it. If something is said often enough, eventually you will begin to believe it. Some mean it. Based on my personal many years of experience in this system, most do not.

What I would like my readers to know is that I have days I myself become confused as to my rights working with the DDSN adult foster care system. I, who consider myself to be a hardworking, law-abiding, tax-paying citizen. Yet, I became uncertain relative to rights of privacy within my own home. Okay forget privacy, just the right to believe that I could be secure and comfortable within my home. As I've heard said by so many, I like to feel as if I'm, "the master of my domain."

That being said, in my home if for any reason I feel the need to communicate with you that a particular procedure makes me feel some kind of way—nervous, anxious, or uncomfortable even—I am of the belief that the thoughts I have conveyed are to be considered. After all it is my home.

We all know that the people we're serving have "rights." They have the right of choice, to say yes, or no. A right to say they don't know. The right to privacy, etc. The *rights* factor has been verbally confirmed time and time again. It would not be inconceivable for me to believe that if Alec has the *right to*, so do I. A time came, however, when clearly my opinion relative to this subject was not being considered at all.

Often the knights would remind me of their right to count clothing or complete home inventory. They insisted on a procedure that included going into my refrigerator, something about temperature control. They further conversed with me regarding the authority of the fire Marshall during in-house inspection, and at one time they were requesting to come in and inspect Alec's bed sheets.

Let me say that I certainly understand that guide lines, regulations, criterion, etc. often are set, and that they need to be maintained. That being stated, we are all individuals with different likes, dislikes, fingerprints, DNA, etc.

When first they came and requested of me that I consider giving Alec a home, none of these procedures were brought to my attention for my consideration.

Regulations regarding procedures are generally put in writing. Normally, there is a regulations handbook for licensing procedure, specific to the community training home one. The dept of DDSN would at times advise that although there are across the board licensing regulations relative to the cth1 program, the providers have liberty to issue more stringent practices if they're deemed necessary.

Due to provider lead-way, realistically not all caregivers had to deal with certain buffoonery. I concluded this after having several conversations with caregivers administering the same service less the nonsense of in-home inventory. Some of these caregivers had concerns relative to the adult foster care program; but no one had requested to come into the caregiver's home and inspect the serviced individuals bed linens.

LORD, fight against those who seek after my soul without a cause. They have hid a net for me in a pit. Unawares make them to fall into their own net.

I see myself as a straight shooter. *Within reach I am a rule follower.* My business model is to attend to the task more so than joshing around. I am of the persuasion *do what you need to do now, so that you may do what you want to do later.* I haven't always been of this mindset. I don't know when it happened, but at this point in life procrastination is not an option for me.

So having said all that, if you present me with the guidelines, criterion, rules, regulations, or facts of a process or program, this practice allows me the ability to make an informed decision. In other words, for me to make the best choice, I desire all that is known to be aforementioned. Let me reiterate that prior to my family and me being solicited concerning home placement for Alec, no mention was made of any of the practices of home inventory, refrigerator temperature, or bed linen inspections business.

As people, we should try and remain focused on what we're about as much as possible. Losing focus, as we all know has never been considered positive. What I mean is that I don't know of anyone who would put the statement, "I lose focus," on a resume cover letter. This idea might sound trivial, but it's not. The fix might sound easy, but I beg to differ. The Bible speaks to laboring to rest. More accurately is says, *labor to rest.* A great deal of the time, though, we fell to adhere to this simple command. Rest in GOD. As a result of our failure to properly rest in HIM, we struggle in every day circumstances.

We, instead, have coined the phrase a *waste of time*. Wasting time has become normal. Let me stroll back briefly. The fire marshal's job in my case was to inspect the home because an "intellectually disabled" person living within the home is a "state ward." The State has mandated that a fire marshal inspection be completed. The fire marshal's focus should be on the safety of the disabled individual who lives within the home. This official has no need to veer to the left or right.

In the position of fire marshal, I am certain lies a great deal of responsibility. I assume that a fire marshal doesn't have time to create unnecessary matters of concern. A fire marshal wasting time in my home, displaying what I have referred to as suspect behaviors is unnecessary. More likely than not, someone is in need of a fire marshal but fails to receive the needed service because the marshal chooses to remain at my house debating with me.

People, we need to focus. More importantly, we need to pick and choose or battles carefully. Once we choose to battle, we must establish a strategy of resolve. This allows us the ability to use manpower more effectively. Consider what you would like the outcome to be first. We all want victory. What strategy should we pursue in whatever endeavor to be certain of victory?

I find my thoughts lingering over trails endured in my attempts to work with Alec. As time moved forward, the natural progression of things simply fell in line. By all measures, Alec had become another member of the family. As I would any member of my family, I felt as though I had to protect him as best I was able.

At times, I found myself protecting Alec from the very people who should have been advocating for him. I also believe that at moments the knights portrayed themselves as protecting him from me. Yet he lives with me. Seven days a week, 24 hours a day. The responsibility for his care is on me. *Protecting him from me, really.*

I pondered these matters. I thought to myself, I'm trusted enough to clean his room, cook his meals, attend to all of his doctor's appointments, accompany him to needed urgent care visits, walk the halls of hospitals at 5 a.m., wash his clothing, and all of the other unspoken situations that can occur when care for a person is in your hands. In all the years of working with Alec, not one administrative person has accompanied him to an appointment of any type. But his finances, well that should be safe guarded by someone outside the home. You know, just in case, etc.

In most instances the provider has control of the financial piece of this puzzle. In doing so, they (the knights) determine what is an appropriate purchase for Alec and when it can be made. I recall times when I have requested Alec's income on his behalf only to wait *(of course not without excuse)* for the check to arrive 9 to 10 weeks later.

For me, the implementation of this procedure is unreasonable, and causes unneeded conflict and anxiety as I consider the fact that not one knight has ever reported to doctor's care, the emergency room, an outpatient same-day procedure, or even come to see him during a bout with illness. In all these years, not one.

I can do all things through Christ who strengthens me.

Chapter Six

MOVING FORWARD WITH INTEGRITY

First and foremost, you must establish as a real concept that you are in the business of providing one of God's fellow children with a most-needed service. You have to determine within yourself that in order to maintain a reputable and relevant business that is sustainable, you will need to deal with others in a moral and ethical manner.

Doing this, you will have established what I refer to as a good reputation. Upkeep of this reputation will attract others to you, thereby expanding your business opportunities. Helping other people in need allows for earning an honorable living. When all parties involved are happy, money changes hand. God is seeking to reward those who obey him by providing service to a person in need.

September 24th, 2019: I received a call from Alec's brother (Mr. Arthur), advising me that he would be in town this coming weekend and would be stopping by to visit with his brother.

September 28th, 2019: Alec's three brothers along with his youngest sister did indeed come by and spend time with Alec.

Through my observance of Alec's gestures and countenance, I couldn't help but know that somehow Alec was aware that his siblings were here, and they had come just to see him. Hmm, he is feeling some kind of way right now. Special indeed. The family reunion didn't last long, but what a beautiful experience I have witnessed.

A CHANGING OF DAILY ACTIVITIES

The life that I lead daily is surely changing. The years have swiftly past by, and the young ones are now young adults, making choices for themselves and notifying their parents of decisions they have made. My time is occupied with holding a "gig" outside the home and continuing care for Alec. Outside of a miracle from GOD (*which we know our FATHER in heaven can effect*), he will never graduate to being entirely responsible for his own well-being.

Life goes on, business as usual. Alec attends the workshop daily, Monday thru Friday for approximately 5 to 6 hours a day if the workshop van shows on time to pick him up and drop him off. I have never really understood what Alec does at the workshop. He is always eager to jump on that van when it arrives to pick him up. He is just as eager to get off the van when he gets home every evening.

By all accounts, Alec seems to be living what some would refer to as a fulfilled life. Not because he enjoys attending a workshop but due to all the different mechanics that are a part of the norm of his life and have been for some time now.

I am not in the professional position to say with a 100 percent certainty that Alec loves the life he lives; however, the out-loud laughter that so often comes from him, the rocking from side to side to include a big smile with all of his teeth exposed, laughing out loud in the wee hours of the morning, patting his feet on the floor, extending his hand out to one of us so that he can be tapped five, these demonstrated attributes afford me the ability to ascertain that Alec loves the life he is living.

Though it may be a bit more difficult to gauge, like all of us, Alec might have ups and downs, ins and outs, good days, and bad days, but his tenacity is immeasurable.

Even with the magnitude of his limitations—and now, because of the time that has gone by, the aging factor needs to be included—he continues to live a rewarding lifestyle.

Chapter Seven

CAREGIVING IN PANDEMIC 2020

Now we are in the error of a new decade, the beginning of a new year. Matters appeared to be moving forward as usual, though seemingly faster and faster as the days went by. Then, suddenly and without remedy or warning, coronavirus happened upon the earth, the month of March in 2020, or at least that's when everything began to change for my household. More specifically, March 16th, 2020. That was when I took notice of the public panic, panic brought about by the virus called Covid-19 a name invented for the novel coronavirus.

In Covid-19's immediate surge, I re-called it being a humorous topic especially among the teenage/young adult community. Parties and gatherings were being name *"Rona Virus"* or *"The Rona,"* of course all in the name of humor. Then the death toll started going up. These numbers continued to rise with no decline in sight.

Hospitals were overwhelmed with not enough beds to hold those who had contracted the virus. Shortages emerged of hospital equipment (ventilators) necessary to help nurse the sick back to health. Frontline responders had no time to rest from having to deal with their patients. Medical professionals began to be infected, some succumbing to the virus. This situation sent out shock waves and fear.

Now we had a shortage of healthcare professionals to treat those sick among us. This virus was responsible for people losing love ones to the right and left of them. It was heart wrenching to witness the death toll rising daily. To aid in combating the virus and limit its spread, jobs began shutting down, with restaurants, day programs, and schools closed. The natural hand shake had been tossed. Social distancing, fist pumps, and the better-preferred elbow jive were implemented, and wearing facial masks in public was mandated. None of this did Alec have any comprehension of.

Please understand that when caring for the mentally fragile, the primary caregiver is responsible for the person's well-being to a great degree (or at least in most cases that's how we feel). Since we have no accurate measure, therefore the phrase "reasonable degree" will be the rationale in this chat for all intents and purposes. Now, for a person who is mentally fragile, note this fact: When the world catches a cold, the mentally fragile catches bronchitis. And for individuals such as Alec, who is a mentally fragile, deaf, non-verbal, legally blind, and diabetic, they catch pneumonia. I had to do everything imaginable and more to keep him healthy and well in the era of the pandemic. I could not pretend his care. Caring for him had to be done.

The pandemic caused me to have to micro manage everything in my efforts to help Alec maintain good health and avoid Covid. Alec had previously established the practice of good hygiene, washing his hands regularly, utilizing hygiene antiseptics, and bathing daily. However, during the pandemic era Alec would need assistance with washing his hands thoroughly and antiseptics had to be used vigorously and more frequently. We included in Alec's routine simple stretching exercises.

As a family we focused more on the consumption of healthier cuisine, this included drinking herbal teas daily, Oolong, Elderberries, Beverage of Ban Lan Gen, Vitamin C, Cucumber white, and so forth.

Solitude came a long and partnered with Covid. At the fore front of the virus Alec refused to wear a mask. His refusal to wear and maintain a mask placed even more limits on what he could do for social interaction. To keep me from consistently handing the mask to him he would simply destroy it. The notion of Alec comprehending the implemented six feet apart strategy was not working for him.

I was aware Alec did not desire to wear a mask. I didn't want to wear a mask either, but I had determined that Covid was not going to come near our dwelling. Certainly not because preventative tactics weren't implemented to keep it out. Alec needed, I needed, and the entire family needed to remain healthy.

Within time Alec had accepted the exercise, and began cooperating with the request to put on a mask. I no longer found myself searching for or picking up mask particles off the floor.

The pandemic caused community activity to halt immediately. Movie theaters, dance halls, restaurants, nail salons, barbershops, and the day activity workshop program Alec attended. Without much of a notice someone had to be home with Alec. We needed to come up with a plan quick. It was very difficult in fact, for me, it was stressful. Our schedules had to be manipulated in a way so that while the day program remained closed a member of the household would always be available for Alec. There was no way to have foreseen this situation coming. It was concluded that household members would simply take turns making themselves available for Alec. Eventually, I was given the opportunity to work from the house. Being given the option to work from home was a blessing for everyone involved. This blessing was not in disguise. I knew it was my Heavenly FATHER doing it again for me and the family.

Those Community Training Home One—CTH (1)-consumers who tested positive for the virus had to be attended to. The responsibility of caring for the consumer is solely on the DSP. Covid was not pretending. In addition, prior to Covid-19, a consumer being hospitalized for any reason becomes an additional daily obligation for the caregiver.

The responsibility of open communication with medical professionals, and the daily upkeep and oversight of the consumer
generally fell to the caregiver's shoulder. State-licensed providers
have implemented within some of the contracts that if the primary
DSP was unable to spend nights at the hospital with the service
consumer, they would not be compensated for the time a consumer
was an inpatient. Of course, I felt this option was ludicrous!

Again, I believed the right parties needed to be put on notice.
This demand was being impressed upon me as a DSP, due to lack
of oversight by the state as to what these providers are permitted to
do with taxpayer's money. Caregivers have entire families to watch
over. From the beginning, I made no secret of the fact that if faced
with this ultimatum I would not have been able to comply.

In over twenty years I have had to go to the emergency room
several times, I have had to attend early morning hours, same day
procedures, and tons of doctor's appointments, and not one time
has any provider's representative even so much as come to see how
Alec was doing. Not one time.

Let's give the preceding a bit of thought. I am a CTH (1) caregiver,
a direct service professional, or DSP in a residential setting. The
short of the long of it is that I have agreed to take a person into my
home and take care of him within the confines of my home. I've
agreed to help him live life in a better way. In other word's improve
his lifestyle to the best of my ability.

At the same time, I have a family I also have a responsibility to
take care of. I 'm missing in action if I'm at the hospital all night,
each night that a consumer has an inpatient stay.

The question I asked was: *What is the state licensed provider paid
to do?* If they administrate finances concerning the consumers, then
it seemed to me that an obligation of the state licensed provider
would be to make certain a consumer had a professional sitter,

for inpatient stay, should it be necessary. This type of assistance is different for everyone, depending on the "level" of the person you have agreed to assist. For Alec, had an inpatient stay occurred, this type of assistance would be needed.

Once someone has agreed to work with a mentally fragile person, the caregiver should treat that person as family. A family function might be slightly different for every household, so the person that the caregiver works with would need to select the caregiver, the family, and the home. The primary caregiver should also have a choice as to who is selected for placement within their home. Both parties should desire to fit together, somewhat like pieces in a puzzle.

If the individual that the caregiver has interviewed with doesn't seem to enjoy certain hobbies or habits practiced by the household, they don't fit in there. For example, if a caregiver participates in frequent church activities but the consumer doesn't enjoy church, that fact should weigh in a decision to move forward with this person as a candidate for residential support. Another example might be if the caregiver is not a smoker and the person being considered for placement is a smoker, both parties should take this fact into account when proceeding.

In regard to my family and Alec, unbeknownst to us, here was the case of a hand and the perfect glove. My family frequents church activities. Alec enjoys going to church. This is evident in his cooperation when preparing to go, and during church service. Alec is a non-smoker, and this is a non-smoking household. For Alec and me, a perfect combination.

I was, in fact, not privy to a great deal of information when I agreed to work with our friend. I have come to recognized that my situation with Alec was ordained by a hire authority.

I should mention for those intending to do this work that all pertinent information isn't going to be revealed in one meeting.

Caregivers who want to take a person into their home should be certain to review plan records for all possible impediments and ask questions. Once a seemingly appropriate match is found, though, both parties may then be interested in moving forward with the possibility of making a placement request, or an application for a respite or honeymoon.

A respite/honeymoon (different entities may refer to it under other names) occurs when involved parties agree for the consumer to come and temporarily stay in the home so they can get to know one another. The stay is for a short period of time with an agreed-upon compensation for that time.

Some providers will try and talk you into a weekend period for the respite or honeymoon. If caregivers are okay with that then by all means they should proceed. I would suggest, however, trying a week or seven days at a minimum, being mindful that seven days isn't a great deal of time. That length of time, however, will provide the caregiver with additional insight into the client concerning behaviors/habits, likes, dislikes, etc. The respite/honeymoon is a great opportunity to see how the immediate family interacts with the consumer in the home.

Once the agreed-upon respite/honeymoon time has ended, then the consumer returns to their original residential supports. If all parties involved agree to move forward with a placement, then a financial plan needs to be completed to include the monthly room /board fees (rent). The rate should be reasonable and customary. Room and board fees are paid for by the consumer through their personal funds.

Depending upon the serviced persons level of understanding, they may have their personal funds in their possession. Usually someone who is capable of handling the financial responsibility of their life can function more independently. Placing that person within a CTH

(1) for assistance wouldn't be necessary. But that being said, most CTH (1) candidates have selected or should have a Representative Payee for oversight of their finances. This subject is sensitive as some providers that have taken on the responsibility of Rep Payee have not been selected by the serviced person.

A situation of this nature can be of concern for many different reasons. For now, let's talk about how it can all work together smoothly. If a Rep Payee, a DSP, and the consumer keep each other abreast on wants, desires, needs, rationale, and decisions, regarding the person being served, all is usually well. On the other hand, if communication is broken or misleading, and lacking consideration of the preferences of the person served, the situation will not run as smoothly as all would prefer.

If circumstances arise and the consumer is unable to pay the room/board fee, the licensed provider is responsible for payment in lieu of the consumer payment. (Note) Providers will try to negate their responsibilities in these matters if allowed. The procedure is the provider is responsible to pay the consumers monthly room/board and collect their money when the consumer is in a position to pay. At no time should a caregiver be allowed to wait on room/board due to the consumer's lack of funds

A stipend negotiated between the licensed provider and the caregiver is also paid to the caregiver. The amount should be based on the care level of the serviced individual/client. Generally, stipends are issued monthly or bi-monthly (twice a month), depending upon the contract provider. Some providers offer choice as to when you prefer to received your compensation. Be sure to ask questions beforehand regarding payment practices. Stipend money comes from the state or federal government and/or private donations.

The room/board fee and stipend are usually paid separately. Though I'm not sure why a provider would select to issue these funds together, I've been advised that some administer the two payments simultaneously monthly. This dual process can only be implemented when the licensed provider also serves as Rep Payee.

The monetary flow is from the federal government, to the state entity, to the state license provider. Stipends are issued from the license provider to the contracted direct support professional /caregiver. Although the funds are released from the state to the license provider the negotiated contract that the DSP/caregiver is expected to sign is an agreement between the licensed provider and the DSP/caregiver. State-required mandates should be adhered to. Ultimately, the oversight of a mandate is governed by the license provider. The room/board is issued from the serviced person personal funds.

DSPs will probably never feel as though they are fully compensated for the excellent service they provide. But remember the Father in heaven sees and is the ONE who renders rewards for diligence and service. This service is a blessing on both ends of the candlestick.

NEGOTIATIONS

If circumstances arise and the consumers level of care changes, the caregiver will revisit the contract for renegotiation. If the thought of compensation not being enough for rendered care becomes a never-ending cycle, the DSP may want to consider pursuing a different avenue of work. The caregiver would be better off using their abilities, gifts, and talents, elsewhere. Living a life of agony, anxiety, or regret is not an edifying pursuit in any respect.

Chapter Eight

TRANSPARENCY IN A PANDEMIC

For me, (I hope this isn't taken out of context, as I'm sure most had some type of stress during this time), the pandemic was rather stressful. Especially when my thoughts went to how the pandemic managed to have shined and even brighter light on exactly how big a *con* was being run on me by the provider. Workshops closed (understandably so), and I experienced a lack of house goods supplies, and an increase in the cost of living, plus solitude, and the added responsibility of keeping Alec safe in regard to the virus, and so forth.

I understood that some state license providers chose to issue CAREs act support funds to their DSPs in recognition of their front-line service during the pandemic. I wasn't a recipient of CAREs act funding relative to my frontline support of Alec. I'm glad I recognize that my heavenly Father is always aware and because HE cares, He will issue the bonus.

As I have previously pointed out, the DDSN license providers have never been supportive throughout our caregiver/provider relationship. The atmosphere has always seemingly appeared to be one of "them against us." I believe that the pandemic simply underscored just how the providers licensed by DDSN do little to nothing for the individuals who are CTH (1) supported.

Respite has always been a scarcity. At least according to the state licensed providers. Yet rest is a necessity, the necessary defense against burnout. Alec has not had a period provided (giving me respite) since somewhere around the end of 2019. Even when I pursued it, as I have for the past twenty years, the state licensed provider rarely has involved themselves with securing respite for Alec. They do, though, release paperwork relative to respite that has an appearance of their involvement, and acknowledges responsibility for payment of the invoice.

Monetary supports for obtained/secured respite services are administered through the license provider. It is in addition to any stipend consideration. This facet of the relationship is also negotiated. For the contracted DSP/caregiver, the agreed stipend amount and the number of respite support days are negotiated.

The procedure on how respite supports are administered can differ, depending on the licensed provider's contract. Some providers issue respite compensation directly to the DSP/caregiver for payment of services, other providers issue compensation directly to the respite provider. I've seen the respite number range from 16 to 30 days annually, or per fiscal year. The rate for respite services normally is based on the consumer care level. The rate is negotiated between the license provider and the servicing individual or organization.

Guidelines exist concerning respite providers and respite supports in general. The licensed provider that services Alec require(s) all respite providers be licensed through the state DDSN. Some providers will not allow the carry over of unused respite days into a new fiscal year. In that same breath, they will let you know that they are unable to provide you any respite services as they do not have any respite caregivers available to do this.

Providers appear to be making rules that financially better their position. That's called business. In this case, consumers and the DSP suffer the consequences of the providers' decisions. This practice has a hint of the impropriety of abuse/exploitation.

If the help you provide is not the help I need, it's not help.

For me and Alec, services of this sort has often been acquired in a creative fashion, a form of "give me one this time, I'll give you two next time." By the point of which I'm finished *wheeling and dealing*, I'm tired- too tired to enjoy the respite I worked so hard to secure. It can be mentally exhausting.

On different occasions, I have made DDSN aware of the lack of respite support, to no avail. In defense of DDSN, people serving in "prominent" positions there seemingly appear to resign without hesitation. Long-term staffing appears to be something of the past. Although I'm not certain, this development could be stress related. Apparently neither the provider nor DDSN is able to keep staff long term as in days past.

Each time an employee resigns from a position, knowledge regarding that position can be lost. When these things happen fast, generally no conscious effort is made to retain important facts or much needed information. Accountability vanishes as well, until none remains.

How is such a "business" as the provider being allowed to make decisions that affect others negatively while simultaneously improving their financial position with that same decision? In all fairness, if the provider is not currently able to provide support services by way of respite, paying the caregivers for the respite services that the provider isn't in the position to supply would only be right.

If another person tells me how much they appreciate what I do without showing me by way of support in ways that make a difference to me and Alec, I might say something not very nice. I have days when I wonder who these people think they are dealing with. Does anyone realize how long they been saying that to me? Probably 40 years out of the 20 years I have been in relationship with this program.

Obtaining Respite supports has always been a crapshoot. Planning a mental break, a quick getaway, or a moment to yourself just to sit in the quiet of the evening is generally pretty impossible. Planning a vacation even in advance has always been like shooting dice, and I don't like to gamble. The subject of respite pertaining to this CTH (1) is a "sore spot" or a "delicate issue" either way, something or someone needs to do something about it. The matter has been going on entirely too long.

Currently, I am of the opinion that the system, from the federal government (DHHS), to state (DDSN), on down—primarily the six-figure income individuals, who get paid for what they know and not what they do are exploiting the people I care for as well as people like me (the caregiver).

Let me give an example. The taxpayers supply the money to support our mentally handicap. Those tax dollars should be used in the most appropriate manner possible to help the mentally fragile to the extinct of which they cannot help themselves. In most cases, that requires payment for supportive services. To be monetarily compensated someone must provide a necessary support to the person in question. These supports will be different depending on the person being served.

Now what I see happening is licensed providers supplying duplicated support services stacked on top of each other. Each licensed provider is receiving compensation under the pretense that they are affording our mentally fragile with a needed service. Honestly, most of the individuals serviced through CTH(1) that I've had contact with don't have a clue as to what these people do.

Now in the case of Alec, I know he has more understanding than most people recognize. I took only a moment to figure out Alec's level of intellect. Yet he doesn't know in what capacity certain providers should be supporting him. Neither does he know that they are "providers" or what a "provider" happens to be. I don't think that he even cares. From all my years of observing him, his position seems to be "leave me alone"

Alec doesn't know what these people do. He doesn't care what they do. Believe me, providers are aware of this. They talk of Alec having a "choice" or of his "rights" yet they are the very entities that invade his "rights." These invasions have nothing to do with his safety. Providers recognize most authority involved with the administration of the services don't have time to pay attention to certain components. Issues may go unattended to until fiscal responsibility is brought to question.

DDSN providers of every entity, the quality of provided services, the billing of supports for working with our intellectually fragile are all important components. The reality is for the CTH (1) consumer providers' supports are little to none. For the direct support caregiver who attends to the cares of the person they are servicing, 99 percent of supportive services are implemented by and through that caregiver.

This matter of a residential provider, case management provider, licensing provider, fire department, disabilities & special needs (DDSN), the US Department of Health and Human Services (DHHS), all also give consideration to the necessary tools used outside of this arena.

Dealing with these various departments and agencies is a lot to reconnoiter with. To know the system and how to determine who is responsible for which piece of the puzzle is a lot to deal with.

What is more, different pieces of officialdom at times behave as if they have and authority to inconvenience/invade and moreover intimidate a caregiver, the very person responsible for all hands-on servicing of the supported individual.

The mentally fragile supported through the CTH1 have been provided a better way a life while serviced through the system. I also believe that servicing a person in this way makes for a better quality of life for the person delivering such services. The job is not easy. It's not glamorous. It's work. Work rewards.

I, personally, have had to fight the so-call *power* of these programs for years just to exercise Alec's rights. His life style has been a better one due to that struggle, I feel. I intentionally chose to ignore the roars of those who spoke of what has always been. I believe I was able to do so due to a combination of ignorance and what some call stubbornness and/or hard headedness. Either way, I now recognize that GOD has given me certain abilities/attributes to use HIS way and for HIS glory. Although I do admit my Spirit self is in constant battle with my flesh.

Help me LORD. I want to do those things that are pleasing in your sight.

Chapter Nine

A LETTER TO MY FATHER

I praise my heavenly FATHER for HE is worthy of all Praise. HE is deserving of all Honor. All the Glory belongs to HIM. I thank my heavenly Father for being a perfect example of HIS adjective: ambidextrous. YOU are the GOD of this and that. The GOD of all possible. YOU are the administrator of my life. More than deserving to be acknowledged, admired, or reverenced. The only true and living GOD. Providing YOUR Sons and Daughters the strength, fortitude, integrity, wherewithal, stamina, mental stability, and, yes when necessary "bulldog tenacity."

For always being faithful and never leaving me nor forsaking me, providing protection within a pandemic. Sending YOUR word and healing me. JESUS! I praise you for when I call on You in the midnight, I'm not required to leave a voice message. You come see about me. You show up and restore me.

It *should* have been enough that You were beaten, battered, bruised, scorned, humiliated, mocked, sold out, and nailed to a tree: the shedding of your blood, paying my sin debt in full. It *should* have been enough. Nonetheless, you continue to demonstrate your love for all those our FATHER has given you, sitting on the right hand of the thrown of grace in heaven, interceding on my behalf.

One day, someday, I will be privileged to lay my crowns at your feet JESUS. Not only have you paid a debt I owed and could never pay, you still demonstrate your love for me by interceding. Thank you for creating my path of restoration back to "OUR" FATHER in heaven. None other is like you JESUS! Not one.

Thank you, FATHER, for never allowing your word to return to you void, but that it accomplishes everything that you send it to do.

Thank you, FATHER for your goodness. Your kindness. Your mercy. Your grace. Your unmatched love demonstrated for us by way of the cross.

The blood of CHRIST has rendered me righteous in my FATHER'S eyes. The same yesterday, today, and forever. As it was from the beginning, it remains today. Your yea is yea. You don't change on me. I love you for that. I don't care what they say about you, LORD. You love me, and I love you. Thank you, FATHER. You are holy. You are sovereign and you are worthy to be praised!

Chapter Ten

PEACE IN A PANDEMIC

My family and I chose to habitually adhere to taking communion as often as we decided during the "pandemic." We also had many opportunities (which we acted upon) to study GOD's word and discuss HIS word together as a family. We are secure in the promises of GOD. Science is cool. We recognize that GOD has blessed us with science and scientists. GOD has also promise that when we put HIM first, HE maintains us. No plague will come near us. We choose to have peace in HIS promises. Approach HIS thrown with a repented heart and allow the Lord of peace to give you peace.

> *GOD'S Peace surpasses our understanding*

Chapter Eleven

PROTECTION AND PROVISION DURING A PANDEMIC

The fact is not only does the Lord GOD provide for all my needs, HE has promised to give me the desires of my heart, HE is well able to do this because He has placed those desires within me. Further, HE also causes everything I put my hands to, to prosper.

GOD is faithful. HIS promises are yes and amen. Because HE has said it. He will do it. GOD watches over His word. HE is the Master Promise Keeper. Now, through my Savior the LORD JESUS Christ and His finished work on that cross, I have been drafted into the family of GOD.

I am a daughter of GOD the most high, heir and joint heir with JESUS Christ. Let us pause for a moment. Think on what we just said. "Heir and joint heir with JESUS". No greater privilege exists. Made manifest by my acceptance of who Christ is and what He has done for me on the cross. I speak of the shedding of His blood. I am saturated in the blood of my Savior, JESUS. What belongs to Him, belongs to me. Our father in heaven is in love with me.

For our mentally fragile our FATHER in his compassionate, merciful characteristics, and HIS infinite wisdom set grace for them. Their inability to speak belief in JESUS doesn't negate citizenship into heaven. GOD is our provider, and HIS plan often defies human logic.

My GOD supplies all my needs according to HIS riches in glory through CHRIST JESUS.

Chapter Twelve

PROSPERITY AND ELEVATION IN A PANDEMIC

As I view the secular news, morning, afternoon, or evening, its apparent that the agenda of the secular news industry is to bombard the law-abiding, hardworking, tax-paying citizens with doom and more doom. (Sports and the weather report don't have time to include gloom.)

Remove the world from your back pocket. Turn it off. Take a minute or two and look to the heavens. Literally, look up to Heaven. Your help will come from there. Thank on His goodness and the fact that He loves us. GOD loves us. It's evident. Think of the cross. No way that GOD would have allowed HIS Son to be beaten, mocked, bruised, scorned, and sacrificed on a cross, publicly or in any other manner, if HE didn't love us overwhelmingly.

What am I saying? During the "pandemic," I focused on my heavenly Father who I know to be awesome, well able, and highly qualified, exceeding all my expectations. I choose to remember the "pandemic" why? My family and I were blessed prior to the "pandemic," then throughout the "pandemic," blessing abounded within our home. The heavenly Father seemed to be intentionally about showing us who HE is by not only keeping us healthy but also allowing HIS favor to rain down on us.

Despite the media and its rhetoric, I'm certain we weren't the only sons and daughters of GOD who thrived throughout the "pandemic."

Our Father in heaven's will was done for us on earth as it is in heaven. Due to the "pandemic," we have been all the more blessed.

In all honesty, at this stage in my life, I have come to recognize that I need more. I experience what some refer to as an emptiness, a void. Now please do not misunderstand the statement. Abba is good to me and my entire household. But I am in a place where I know that Abba can offer more, and I want to experience that more right here and now.

My heavenly Father has always been and will always be. He stands up, but He doesn't stand still. He is always moving evolving, even though one moment in HIS presence is a blessing, more is always possible.

The LORD gives us the power to prosper. Promotion comes from the heavenly Father. HE uses man as dust to do HIS good pleasure.

Chapter Thirteen
PURPOSE IN A PANDEMIC

We need to know who we are in Christ Jesus and not only know who we are, but act according to what we know. We are allied with a purpose.

We should be grateful for the grace of GOD. We should strive to achieve genuine relationships and be intentional about maintaining these genuine relationships. We always tend to note that family and friends are stress creators. We should more readily note that family and friends take away stress as well.

Recognize when you are stressed, fatigued, exhausted or overwhelmed, and be deliberate seeking out a source of release. Change the way you act or think about matters. Take care of yourself. Improve on yourself, and you will always improve on the care you provide to another. As I have learned contribution to the lives of others make life worth living.

Always remember that money is not everything. In comparison to some of life's provisions, money means nothing. However, money does answer a multitude of issues. Remember nothing is wrong with being monetarily compensated for providing a better quality of life to God's other children. Improving the quality of life for society's most vulnerable is a needed service.

Figure out what is needed, and provide it. Don't let anyone suggest that if you expect pay for your effort, ability, and time, this is the wrong business. That's Con 101. We serve each other every day, all day, and are compensated for the services we provide. Why would that change? Each state may have different pathways into serving their intellectually disabled. Some states may have more than one avenue to do this. If GOD has given you a desire to work with the mentally fragile, pray about it, do your research, and proceed.

While serving in this venue, I have repeatedly had conversation with people who seemed to be interested in serving others in the DDSN/CTH (1) capacity. Please allow me to add that the service is definitely needed. An overwhelming number of mentally fragile people within this system would benefit from much-needed one-on- one service within a family environment. Further, please allow me to add that you will always find some pluses and minuses in every situation if approached correctly. This can be different for each person involved because as detailed in our fingerprints, we are all individuals. Ultimately, the pros outweigh the cons.

Over a period of 20 years in an effort to recruit CTH (1) caregivers, I used mounds of scrap paper to dictate notes and telephone numbers. I handed out the business cards of others. I have attempted to educate people on how to get started during conversations at church, a doctor's office, public parks, and so on. I've handed notes to sons to forward to their mothers within financial institutions. On and on it goes.

Feeding important information in this manner doesn't allow for a great deal of follow-through. While this might sometimes be necessary, following through can be awkward or difficult. My effort is to assist all interested persons, no matter on which side of the fence. I try to help people obtain needed information regarding assisting a system that definitely needs the assistance. I try to help people improve the life and lifestyles of others who may desire a lifestyle change.

I know of no better way to do the above but to write about the experience as I have tried to do here. I will add that everyone's experience can and will be somewhat different. But reading what I have set down will definitely guide those interested, in the right direction.

These days we hear the word "transparency" a lot within the U.S. Department of Health & Human Services or DHHS (the federal government), Department of Disabilities & Special Needs or DDSN (the state government), as well as local providers licensed through DDSN. My advice is to disregard the lip service and ask questions, seek details. If you still do not get satisfaction, ask again. Ask the same party or a different party. Keep asking until you are given an answer that makes sense to you.

This answer may not always be the one you're hoping for. Once you have received an answer and your understanding of the answer is made whole, though, you will have learned something. Pass that learning forward or work toward the development of what you believe to be a better method of resolving an issue. You will soon began understanding that those who have answers to the questions you ask are far and few between.

A great deal of time people in officialdom are not fully abreast regarding all avenues as to process. You will also begin to see that actually no single answer exists, but depending on the situation right answers or responses can differ because we're talking about people. People are different and differing avenues can be taken to arrive at what individuals would call "success."

We may all have the same destination (a better lifestyle experience), but different methods are utilized to obtain that better lifestyle. The Community Training Home One-CTH (1) is just one of the many methods offered to service our mentally/intellectually fragile; however, in reference to residential supports it seems to be the best.

Now, what is more, while the CTH (1) is a very good service help-ing to improve the lifestyle of our intellectually/mentally fragile. the program is not for everyone. Having an extra bedroom in your house is not a qualifier for the direct care profession, no more than the diagnosis of mentally/intellectually disable is an automatic qualifier for services within the CTH (1). A potential caregiver should have a desire to help improve the life of another. The other may have a desire to experience life from within a different capacity-within a home.

More than a single motive may well be in play, but I will only mention a primary one. This position is one of service, and at times it comes with sacrifice. When you have determined that you have a desire to serve our mentally fragile by means of residential supports, start by contacting the DHHS or the DDSN or the local state house. States may have these sectors under slightly different names. Primarily, the point of contact will be the Department of Disability and Special Needs (DDSN).

Each state may have different recommendation and/or guidelines for pursuit. Some states may require a license, while others may not. Some may require continued education courses or annual classes, as well as house inspections, announced and unannounced. Programs within the same state may have different criteria or rules established regarding contracting with its specific program.

The responsibility of the individual that is pursuing a residential direct support opportunity of this type is to seek out these provid-ers and interview them. These interviews allow the department the opportunity to determine what the candidates are willing to subject themselves to in supporting our mentally fragile within a CTH (1) category.

These interviews also open the avenue to discuss money matters. Yes money-what the contracted rate of pay will be for the service you are providing. What determines the contracted rate, and so on. In essence, the federal government views this service as foster care. This consideration allows the administered compensation to be federally tax exempt, which many deem as a perk. Consider the information carefully. Also consider the state stance on the subject of taxation relative to foster care.

The interview process is an opportunity to discuss all things important to you concerning the program. It's an opportunity to learn. You may determine within yourself that you are better equipped to journey forward and establish a CTH (1) program as a license provider recruiting a team of CTH (1) caregivers to work under your umbrella.

I don't suggest, however, that you jump in that deep. Not to start off anyway. If you've had previous work experience with our mentally fragile in a residential capacity and you decide that you would like to serve in the role of a license provider administering your own program, throw your hat in the ring. Your help is needed. Don't let anyone or anything detour you from that goal.

Along with that, let me suggest that you tread lightly. Remember, we have no shortage of lessons to learn serving our mentally fragile in a residential capacity. By now, I'm sure you've noticed that I use the word serve or service a great deal. That's because in this profession I have envisioned myself as a server. It helps me to stay focused.

I'm of the opinion that most in this profession do well to view themselves on the frontline always as serving first. Working with our intellectually fragile individuals in a residential capacity of any sort is important function. However, serving our intellectually fragile within the CTH (1), residential arena takes the importance of that service up a notch, or two.

Residential supports are a needed service. Residential supports within the CTH (1) means huge responsibility. Much of the time the situation can be a one-on-one. Primary direct service professionals have the awesome obligation to seek out and provide lifestyle methods that are aimed at improving the life experience of others, with their blessing. The benefits of these obligations are outstanding.

Set aside those obligations for a moment and let's consider some implications. The caregiver has the obligation of assistance with healthcare. As the primary DSP it is your responsibility to assure the maintenance of healthcare is adhered to accordingly-mentally, physically, and spiritually. Rising suddenly at any hour before daybreak due to the occurrence of an unexpected illness is never pleasant, no matter who the sufferer happens to be. When dealing with our intellectually fragile, recall a previous statement of mine: When America catches a cold, the intellectually fragile catches a bronchitis/pneumonia.

Those who work with the mentally fragile discover a definite blessing, so be intentional about placing matters in their priorities. Examine yourself thoroughly. This helps you to determine your motives and gives you a chance to put the motives in order.

If I am to be given an opportunity to rate the official system of operation of this work based solely on my personal experience, with a numbered rating of 1 through 5, the numeral 1 being the best, top rated, and 5 the worst, or at the bottom, let's move forward. You are probably already aware that when it comes to concerns and oversight of our consumers by the system that is ultimately responsible relative to care/upkeep of the people served, my opinion is that oversight is way over the top on one end and never enough on that other end.

Some within the DDSN administration maybe sincere in their efforts but often those efforts are short or shallow with many pieces to this puzzle. So be mindful and pick and choose your battles carefully. Be strategic. Pursue certain concerns only during an election season. Often the results of concern in this season are dealt with swiftly. Rectified immediately. No further action, case closed, etc. Outside of election year, conclusions come at a slow pace.

No worries. The situation could be worst. I viewed similar DDSN systems working with the mentally fragile in foreign lands. When I say it could be worst, believe me, it could.

Once you decide to step up and enter this profession, you create another opportunity for improvement to the system.

Let every man examine himself

Chapter Fourteen

DEPARTURE AFTER A PANDEMIC

Twenty years plus some have passed. Changes have occurred within the system of things as we have known it and throughout society. I don't want to blame what has happened on coronavirus/Covid-19 and all its variants, though the pandemic has taken its toll. I will note that the virus, and other events played their part in spearheading the recognition and direction we're seemingly moving toward as a nation, and for that matter in this world.

Let's not forget that Alec and me both have aged twenty plus years from our initial introduction. Alec moves much slower than in times past and I'm not that swift myself.

Technology and all the ambience it created over the years has had its pluses and minuses. When I look around, I see that our heads are bowed. But not to give thanks to our Creator. Instead, to give credence to that world we hold in our hands: the mighty cell phone. People don't even acknowledge one another in passing. The world appears to be tired.

I find myself needing to be honest with my social comrades, family, and at times myself. From the start in my outreach work of service, my only thought was to provide a home for Alec, and somehow prove my existence to be of satisfactory value. Caring for him help me establish a feeling of self-worth. At moments I found myself feeling shame because of that motive. Yes, assisting him in improving his lifestyle allowed me to enjoy a feeling of value.

Contributing to Alex life has made my own life worth living. I recognize this is a real world, and we live real lives. I needed to do some maturing. Hard work and the passage of time allowed me to mature. I no longer feel any shame for my original motive.

Alec has experienced a fuller life in a way he could have never imagined outside of his inclusion within this family. He proves this assessment to be the real thing by the ceaseless out-loud laughter, rubbing of the back of his head, and the pitter pat of his feet on the floor.

I know these actions are indication of his joy, pleasure, and happiness.

I also know that he should not be branded by his cognitive limitations, which I've concluded Alec employs in some degree as a mechanism of defense. Don't call him retarded. He is not retarded. He is the family we chose.

At certain times my heart wrenches at the thought of someday concluding the family relationship with him as we all know it. Departing with him will not be easy. Alec has become a part of us. For him it would mean having to locate another family and familiarize himself with a new environment.

I'm not sure as to exactly how much longer my relationship with Alec will remain in this role. I know change is inevitable. Meanwhile I will look to the heavens for guidance concerning the shift and trust that the heavenly FATHER will make it alright.

GOD knows that I've cared for Alec over twenty years.

THE END

GLOSSARY OF ACRONYMS

DDSN: Department of Disabilities & Special Needs
DHHS: Department of Health & Human Services
DSP: Direct Service Professional and/or Caregiver
CTH (1): Community Training Home (1)
Rep Payee: Representative Payee

CPSIA information can be obtained
at www.ICGtesting.com
Printed in the USA
BVHW031914141022
649470BV00012B/1625

9 780996 799737